not alone

Cultivating gospel rich community and intentional discipleship

A DEVOTIONAL BIBLE STUDY ON THE BOOK OF II TIMOTHY

cas monaco

Thru A Dirty Window
501 Finsbury St. #303
Durham, NC 27703

www.thruadirtywindow.wordpress.com
www.facebook.com/thruadirtywindow

1st printing, January 2013

Cover Design and Layout: Michal Rudolph Designs

All Scripture
New American Standard Bible
Reference Edition,
LaHabra: A.J. Holman Company, 1960.

to faithful followers of Jesus Christ:

MAY YOU TAKE WHAT YOU LEARN HERE

AND PASS IT ON TO THE

NEXT GENERATION

contents

DISCIPLESHIP—WHAT IS IT? 9

THE GOSPEL—A CALL TO FOLLOW 27

CHARACTERISTICS OF A DISCIPLE 47

BEWARE! 69

BE READY! 89

FIX YOUR EYES ON THE PRIZE 109

*Thank you faithful women of
Summit Church for all of your
sacrifice, enthusiasm, and support.
Without you this would
never have happened.*

Discipleship – What Is It?

Discipleship – What Is It?

By making the choice to engage in this six week study on the topic of discipleship, chances are you're eager to build into the lives of other believers, you're longing for someone to build into your life, or perhaps a little bit of both. It is my prayer that by participating in this study, you will deepen your relationship with Jesus Christ, which in turn will impact your relationship with others around you.

Christ-centered community is integral to our growth in Christ, and discipleship takes that community to a deeper level. By taking a step of faith to open the pages of this study, you also demonstrate the courage you need to expose the details of your life and heart to another believer. The Lord quite often uses *our* experiences to spur another believer's faith or uses the affliction of a friend to give *us* courage.

What is discipleship? Dietrich Bonhoeffer, renowned Christian and martyr for Christ states that discipleship is essentially "Jesus Christ and Jesus Christ alone; the sole content of discipleship is to "follow Christ."[1] Essentially speaking, following Christ is what this study is about. At the same time, it will provide instruction on how to encourage others to do the same. However, we must understand that following Christ is not an easy venture, nor one to be taken lightly. The more deeply we understand who He is, the greater claim He will have on our lives.

The Bible is God's revelation to mankind; it's His Word that exalts Jesus Christ as King and reflects His heart for His children and for the nations. The apostle Paul in this letter to his disciple Timothy writes, "All Scripture is inspired by God, and is profitable for teaching, for reproof, for correction, for training in righteousness, that the man (or woman) of God may be adequate, equipped for every good work" (II Timothy 3:16-17). Eugene Peterson urges us to recognize the power of God's revealed Word,

> "This Scripture text, in the course of revealing God, pulls us into the revelation and welcomes us as participants in it. What I want to call attention to is that the Bible, all of it, is **livable**; it is the text for living our lives. It reveals a God-created, God-ordered, God-blessed world in which we find ourselves at home and whole."[2]

[1]Dietrich Bonhoeffer, *Dietrich Bonhoeffer—Discipleship, Vol. IV* (Augsburg Fortress, 2005), 4.
[2]Eugene Peterson, *Eat This Book* (Eerdmans, Grand Rapids, 2006), 18.

Therefore, the foundation of this study will rest on the Word of God, and while we will focus primarily on II Timothy, we will see that the whole canon of Scripture works together to point us to Christ.

You will be encouraged to read II Timothy many times throughout this study, which will help you grasp the context of the book as a whole. In fact, I encourage you to read it every day, and as you do, the truths will embed themselves in your heart, which will allow the Holy Spirit to use them to deepen your relationship with the Lord. Each lesson is broken down into five days to help give some structure and breathing room as you study. The questions on Day Five will be used for small group discussion. They are not new questions, but instead are taken from the week's study. Additionally, I'll include some basic Bible study principles that will help you in the future as you study the Word on your own.

The first half of this guidebook will focus on Jesus Christ and what it means to be His disciple, and the second half will focus on what it looks like to participate in what is often called Jesus' great commission: "Go, therefore into all the world and make disciples..."(Matthew 28:19). The format will guide you through time in the Word on your own, which will prepare you for group discussion. Obviously the more time and effort you put in, the more you will gain from and contribute to the small group time. The eventual goal is summed up best in II Timothy 2:1-2: "Be strong in the grace that is in Christ Jesus. The things that you heard from me in the presence of many witnesses, these entrust to faithful men who will be able to teach others also."

PRAY

Take some time, before you move into the study itself, and pray. Talk to the Lord about what you hope to gain from your study of II Timothy. If you have a sense of anticipation, talk to Him about why. If you're feeling reluctant, lay out your reasons. If you feel uncertain or that you're in over your head, ask Him to give you faith to take the next step. Pray that He'll use His Word in your life. Thank Him for the freedom and opportunity you have to gather with others who want to grow, and ask Him to reveal more of Himself to you over the next six weeks.

day one

1. What do you think it means to be a *disciple* of Christ, and why?

2. a. What compels you to participate in a study on discipleship. What do you hope to gain and what hesitations (if any) do you have as you begin?

   b. If you are hesitant, fearful and/or reluctant, ask the Lord to help you understand why.

3. Who has influenced you the most spiritually, and why?

4. Read II Timothy all the way through. From now on the reminder to read through the book will be at the beginning of each "day" of study. For today, just read it, and Day Two will guide you through the step of *observation*.

REFLECTION

As you wrap up your study today go back to question #2. Ask the Lord to help you with your feelings as you begin. If you have a sense of anticipation—tell Him that. Ask Him to help you hear His voice and respond to His Word. Thank Him for providing the opportunity to study II Timothy. If you are feeling hesitant or reluctant—lay everything out on the table before Him. Ask Him to help you understand the root of your feelings and then to give you insight into your fears as you study His Word.

day two

Wait to read II Timothy until you get to the "Book Summary" part of today's study.

Eugene Peterson, again, compels us to draw near to the Lord through the Word: "This rich, alive, personally revealing God as experienced in Father, Son, and Holy Spirit, addressing us in whatever circumstances we find ourselves, at whatever age we are, in whatever state we are—me, you, us. Christian reading is participatory reading, receiving the words in such a way that they become interior to our lives, the rhythms and images becoming practices of prayer, acts of obedience, ways of love."[3] So, today we are going to dip our toes into II Timothy to get a feel for the book. However, let us remember that each time we open up the Scriptures we encounter the triune God through His living Word. Let's pray that He will "open our eyes that we may behold wonderful things from His law" (Psalm 119:18).

BOOK SUMMARY

Whenever you take on a book of the Bible, an important first step is to get an idea of the whole book, a "fly-by" to give you an idea of the big picture of the overall message and structure of the book. I know from experience that this step can feel intimidating, but press through and ask the Lord for wisdom. It's surprising how much you'll learn by reading it through all at once.

Here's some background that might help as you begin. The apostle Paul penned II Timothy right at the end of his life. The four chapters are Paul's final words to his friend and disciple, Timothy. We'll learn much more about both of these men as we study, but for now, as you read the four chapters, take note of the big idea of each chapter. Look for repeated ideas or an overall theme as you read. Again, don't worry about being "right" or "wrong." Simply make observations.

---

[3]Eugene Peterson, *Eat This Book* (Eerdmans, Grand Rapids, 2006), 28.

As I break down the book for you here. Jot your observations below. Most Bibles indicate "paragraphs" with verse numbers in **bold**. Most of the time these highlights signify a shift in topic, like a paragraph break does for us. Remember, however, chapter breaks, verse references, and verses in **bold** are there to help us and are not part of the original texts of scripture.

1. So, read each chapter all the way through again. As you complete a chapter, make just a few observations—no less than two and no more than six. Look for things like Paul's references to Jesus Christ. What does he emphasize? And, since this is a letter to Timothy, what do you observe about Paul's relationship with Timothy in these four chapters?

II Timothy 1:1-14

II Timothy 1:15-18

II Timothy 2:1-13

II Timothy 2:14-26

II Timothy 3:1-13

II Timothy 3:14-17

II Timothy 4:1-8

II Timothy 4:9-18

II Timothy 4:19-22

2. a. Well done! You've completed what can often feel rather daunting. Before you wrap up your study, what did you notice about Paul's view of Christ as you read?

b. Based upon your observations, what would you say is one thing Paul wanted Timothy to understand?

REFLECTION

You've now read II Timothy all the way through a few times. Take a few minutes and thank the Lord for what He's revealed to you from His Word. Perhaps you've never read through an entire book of Scripture before. Thank Him for the opportunity, for a strong mind that enables you to understand, and healthy eyes to see and read the words. Most of all thank Him for His promise in II Timothy 2:7, "Consider what I say, for the Lord will give you understanding in everything."

day three

Read II Timothy

In their simple, yet comprehensive book, *The True Story of the Whole World*, Craig Bartholomew and Michael Goheen contend that you and I are participants in the grand drama of Biblical history. This real-life drama "begins with God's creation of the universe and human rebellion and runs through the history of Israel to Jesus and on through the Church, moving to the coming kingdom of God. At the very center of this story is the man called Jesus of Nazareth, in whom God has revealed his fullest purpose and meaning for the world. Only this one story unlocks the meaning of human history—and thus the meaning of your life and mine."

Did you notice this powerful phrase? "Jesus unlocks the meaning of human history, and thus the meaning of your life and mine."[4] It's of vital importance that we realize that we're part of a much bigger story. God not only redeems our lives, but He includes us in the grand drama of redemption history. So, we must realize that the book of II Timothy was at first a letter, written by Paul to his son in the faith, Timothy. We know from the context of chapter four that Paul was nearing the end of his life, and this letter is, in effect, his last exhortation to Timothy, who at the time was the pastor of a church in Ephesus. We'll explore the bigger picture of this point in history in the next lesson. Today we're going to explore how Paul and Timothy met and the nature of their relationship.

1. For background on Paul's miraculous encounter with Christ, begin reading in Acts 9:1-30. Notice that Paul was called Saul until Christ transformed him. Summarize what you discover about Saul, his experience on the road to Damascus, and the result.

---

[4]Craig Bartholomew, Michael Goheen, *The True Story of the Whole World: Finding Your Place in the Biblical Drama* (Faith Alive Christian Resources, Grand Rapids, 2004), 12.

2. Continue reading Acts 15:36-16:5. This portion of Scripture gives you a good idea of the transforming power of the Gospel of Christ and the specific way the Lord leads. It was no accident that Paul and Timothy met.

3. According to Acts 16:1-5, what do you learn about Timothy?

4. Scan the following Scripture passages and record the various places Paul and Timothy traveled together, along with some of the activities they were involved in along the way (this isn't comprehensive, but should provide a good overview of their ministry). In addition, make observations about their community.

Acts 16:6-12

Acts 17:1-15

Acts 18:1-5

Acts 20:1-5

These two men (and several others) logged a lot of time together, traveled many miles, and served the Lord together in a variety of intense situations. It's not hard to imagine why their relationship was strong and close.

REFLECTION

We all go through seasons when the Lord surrounds us with great friends who spur us to follow Christ, who exhort us to live for Him above all else. I'm grateful for good friends who have traveled the same path and who model a wholly devoted life. Most of my closest friends, those with whom I've logged the most hours, don't live near me today. However, we all make an effort to touch base: in person, over Skype, or by text or e-mail. I'm very thankful for their influence and their commitment.

What difference does it make in your life to have friends who follow Christ? How can you continue to cultivate and nurture those relationships?

Thank Jesus for the men and women He's placed in your life to encourage you. Pray regularly for each one of them, and set up a Starbucks or Skype date this week and say thanks!

day four

Read II Timothy

The story of Scripture began with God's creation, and the drama of history unfolds with each turn of a page in our Bible. Now, over 2000 years later, we all have a story to tell as well, a story that tells how Jesus Christ intervened and redeemed our hearts and our lives at the point of salvation and how He continues to renew and transform us every single day. We see the transforming power of the Lord in Paul's life as he lays out his call, his passion, his experiences for Timothy. He doesn't sugar coat or hide the difficulties from his friend, but he's brutally honest. Paul has experienced significant fall-out in his ministry. He knows firsthand the reality of persecution, and he's facing death. Central to the stark reality of Paul's difficult circumstances is Jesus Christ. This letter is a testimony to His faithfulness in the face of trying times and a call to guard the treasure of the gospel.

So, the purpose of today's lesson is to give you time to consider your personal history. Take time to reflect on your spiritual journey with Christ and the most significant ways He has impacted your life. I encourage you to give yourself some space and a good chunk of time as you work on your story. I'll provide a variety of questions to help jog your memory, but the best place to begin is in prayer. Ask the Lord to help you remember and to help you put your memories into words.

1. How did you come to know Jesus Christ personally?

Whether you trusted Christ as a young child or an adult, include both how you came to know Christ as your Savior, and also some of the ways in which Christ worked in your life to bring about spiritual growth.
For example: *Maybe you placed your faith in Christ as a small child but didn't start to take Him seriously until you were in high school or college. If that's the case, what happened to bring about that change?*

Was there a situation that revealed a deeper need in your life? If so, how did God meet you?

Perhaps it wasn't until recently that you became a Christian. What were the circumstances that He used to draw you to Himself?

2. How does God continue to work in your life now? Note lessons that you continually need to learn, or describe ways that He shows His grace in your life. Include verses or passages from the Bible that He has used to encourage you.

3. How has He used other believers to build your faith? Describe ways that you've experienced spiritual growth as you've walked with the Lord.

4. What are some of your current longings and desires, and how are you relying on the Lord today?

REFLECTION

I recently finished reading Far As The Curse Is Found, *and I loved the author's description of the way Jesus invaded history: "There is an altogether marvelous quality to the concreteness, the this-worldliness, even the earthiness, of the drama of redemption. This history does not transpire within some ethereal and bloodless realm of perfection. Quite the contrary, the events spoken of in Scripture take place within the same world in which you and I live. The* redemption of Jesus Christ was not worked out in heaven. It all took place right here, in this world, the same world in which you and I rear our children, pay our bills, and shovel our snow-covered walks."[5]

As you recreated your story on the pages of this book, you've described the continuing story of redemption, the absolute reality of Jesus Christ invading your heart and life and making you new! May we never, ever get over the power of the gospel.

Stop and worship. Worship Him for His great love demonstrated for you at the cross. Rejoice that you serve a risen Savior who broke the curse of sin and death and reigns as King.

---

[5]Michael Williams, *Far As The Curse is Found-The Covenant Story of Redemption* (Phillipsburg, P&R Publishing, 2005), 12.

day five

Read II Timothy

These questions are taken from the previous four days and are designed to generate group discussion.

1. What do you think it means to be a ***disciple*** of Christ, and why?

2. What compels you to participate in a study on discipleship, what do you hope to gain, and what hesitations (if any) do you have as you begin?

3. Who has influenced you the most spiritually and why?

4. As you surveyed II Timothy (Day Two), what are two observations you made about Jesus Christ, Paul, and/or Timothy?

5. The passages in the book of Acts (from Day Three) reveal a variety of things about Paul and Timothy's relationship. What did you learn that you didn't know before?

6. How does it feel to know that you're part of the grand story of redemption? What difference does it make in your life, if any?

7. Over the next six weeks, take turns sharing your story.

LESSON TWO

The Gospel – A Call to Follow

The Gospel – A Call to Follow

Bob and I served with Cru's campus ministry in the Soviet Union from 1991-1993. We arrived just months before the U.S.S.R. dissolved into the Former Soviet Union. We were in Moscow when the Soviet flag was lowered for the last time and the Russian flag was raised over Red Square. In the course of the dissolution of the Communist government, the Lord opened a window for the proclamation of the gospel. We were met with such openness and receptivity. Somehow we knew it wouldn't last long, so every day we focused on getting the gospel to as many students as we possibly could from Russia east to the Baltic Republics and west to Central Asia. Often we faced food shortages, endured weeks without hot water (and sometimes without any water), language barriers, and extreme weather. What kept us going was the gospel, and we knew that while living in another culture was a hardship, it was a privilege to proclaim the Good News at a critical point in history.

Living as a missionary afforded us the opportunity to concentrate on one thing, which helped to make life much more simple. Honestly, when I reflect back on those years that focus is what I miss the most—life in the United States and in the 21st Century is complex. As followers of Christ, we are all called to share the gospel, right? Yet, often our focus is, understandably, blurred by the stuff of life: birthday parties, family reunions, job interviews, home maintenance, landscaping, couponing, blogging, a desire to be married, a dysfunctional family, or a rebellious child. The list of things to do is endless, and yet, no matter where we are, no matter our role, no matter the stage of life, the call to every believer remains the same: "Go therefore and make disciples of all the nations, baptizing them in the name of the Father and the Son and the Holy Spirit " (Matthew 28:19). For many of us "going" might mean walking up the path to your neighbor's front door or taking a step of faith with that co-worker. It might mean serving our bedridden spouse, or it could involve being a missionary in a different country. Wherever we live, whatever we do, we are called to make disciples. What does this mean exactly? This lesson will seek to answer that question as we examine Paul and Timothy's relationship and ministry, and as we explore the meaning of "the gospel."

Remember, the grand drama of biblical history "begins with God's creation of the universe and human rebellion and runs through the history of Israel to Jesus and on through the Church, moving to the coming kingdom of God. At the very center of this story is the man called Jesus of Nazareth, in whom God has revealed his fullest purpose and meaning for the world. Only this one story unlocks the meaning of human history—and thus the meaning of your life and mine."[1] In order to maintain a Christ-centered view of life, we must continue to pivot back to the gospel and constantly remind each other that we are part of the much bigger story of history—the story of redemption.

This week's lesson will help us better understand the flow of this true story—the gospel, and give us a glimpse into the apostle Paul's heart as we examine his compelling exhortation, his final words, to his beloved son in the faith. I cannot tell you how encouraging this reminder has been for me at this point in my life as a follower of Christ. It is my prayer it will be encouraging for you as well.

PRAY

Lord, I am so grateful for your Word that is living and actively at work in our hearts. I pray for myself and for those who study it today that we will be changed by our encounter with you. In Jesus' name.

---

[1] Bartholomew and Goheen 12.

Read II Timothy

What is the gospel? The Greek word for gospel is *evangelio* and means "good news" or the "gospel story." Understanding the gospel is critical to our understanding of II Timothy and discipleship. Keller asserts, "The gospel isn't advice: It's the good news that you don't need to earn your way to God; Jesus has already done it for you. And, it's a gift that you receive by sheer grace—through God's thoroughly unmerited favor. If you seize that gift and keep holding on to it, then Jesus's call won't draw you into fanaticism or moderation. You will be passionate to make Jesus your absolute goal and priority, to orbit around him...."[2]

J.D. Greear in his book *Gospel* describes it this way: "The gospel is that Christ has suffered the full wrath of God for my sin. Jesus Christ traded places with me, living the perfect life I should have lived, and dying the death I had been condemned to die...He took my record, died for it, and offers me His perfect record in return. He took my shameful nakedness to clothe me with His righteousness. When I receive that grace in repentance and faith, full acceptance becomes mine. He lived in my place, and then offered to me a gift. Theologians call that 'gift righteousness.'"[3]

The good news of the gospel is wrapped up in the message of salvation and also includes the bigger story of redemption, beginning all the way back in Genesis. So, take a deep breath and pray the Lord will give you mental and emotional space to meet with Him today. Ask Him to use His Word in your heart and life today.

1. Read II Timothy 1:8-14. Pay close attention to the action verbs in these verses, and look for Paul's message to Timothy.

II Timothy 1:8

[2]Tim Keller, *The Kings Cross: The Story of the World in the Life of Jesus,* (Dutton, New York, 2011), 20.
[3]J.D. Greear, *Gospel, Recovering the Power that Makes Christianity Revolutionary* (B&H Publishing, Nashville, 2011), 46.

II Timothy 1:13

II Timothy 1:14

2. As we look at II Timothy 1:9-12 we see different components of the gospel revealed. Most importantly, we learn that God has saved us, called us with a holy calling—not according to our works, but according to His own purpose and grace which was granted to us in Christ Jesus from all eternity.

   a. According to II Timothy 1:10 God has revealed His purpose and grace by the appearing of Christ Jesus. What is the result of Christ's appearing? *(Hint: the answer is right there in the verse)*

   b. Paul describes some of the results of the gospel in II Timothy 1:11-12. What are they and for what reason does Paul willing suffer for the gospel?

3. While the scope of this study doesn't include the Old Testament. It is important that we continue to recognize that by God's predetermined plan and foreknowledge Jesus died and rose again not just for you and me, but for all of mankind. As we learned earlier, "The story of the Bible unlocks the meaning of human history— and thus the meaning of [Paul and Timothy's life] your life and mine."[4]

Compare II Timothy 1:9-12 with Acts 2:22-24 and Acts 3:18-26. What insight do you gain, especially from the Old Testament references, regarding the gospel message from these two passages?

REFLECTION

How does the scope of redemption change your view of the gospel, or why does it matter that the story of the Bible is bigger than our experience?

---

[4]Bartholomew & Goheen, 13.

Read II Timothy

Paul writes from prison, awaiting execution. Take note that his letter rings with a somber and reflective tone. Timothy is a young pastor and his responsibilities are great as he leads believers in the face of an anti-Christian culture and government. Paul, as you will quickly learn, always points him back to the Savior and the gospel.

As followers of Christ in the 21st Century, it is easy to forget that we are part of an over-arching plan of God, and sometimes it is hard to relate to the level of suffering Paul and Timothy faced. However, it is important to recognize that we stand on the shoulders of men and women who endured great suffering for the cause of Christ. Although our circumstances are vastly different, Paul's words to Timothy are as significant for us today as they were for Timothy in the 1st Century because the call to follow Jesus Christ is the same.

Ask the Lord to prepare your heart to receive truth from His Word today.

1. Take a look at the following passages and note the types of things Paul shares with Timothy about himself and his circumstances. Then note what stands out to you the most and why.

II Timothy 1:8

II Timothy 1:15

II Timothy 4:6-7

II Timothy 4:10, 14-18

There is something both disheartening and deeply encouraging about Paul's vulnerability. On the one hand, his circumstances, from a human perspective, have not turned out so well. He suffered hardship and faces death by execution. Most of the men he ministered to and with deserted him. He often felt no support, faced vigorous opposition, and yet held fast to Jesus Christ. Despite intense suffering he saw beyond the pain of his present circumstances to the Lord and the heavenly kingdom. Paul grasped the gospel in the fullest sense, and he clearly longs for Timothy to grab hold of the same.

2. How does it feel to know that you are called to follow Him, no matter your circumstances, and how might this perspective affect your priorities?

3. As I noted earlier, Paul does not sugarcoat his instruction. He is brutally honest about reality; he shares his need, his disappointments, and provides Timothy with a solid example of a man who perseveres in Christ. Why is this level of transparency so important as we develop discipleship relationships?

4. Take a look at the following verses and notice how Paul keeps Christ at the center of his encouragement. As you read each passage, write down the truths about Christ that Paul highlights.

For example: II Timothy 1:8-11, Jesus saved us, called us with a holy calling—even in the midst of suffering I can remember that there's a purpose—one that was granted me in Christ from all eternity.

II Timothy 2:8-10

II Timothy 2: 24-26

II Timothy 3:14-15

II Timothy 4:8, 18

Characteristically, Paul always keeps Christ the focus of his message. Christ captured his heart on the road to Damascus and he was forever changed. I love how he constantly reminds Timothy of the gospel. Christ is Paul's rallying point, his source of motivation, and the very reason why he endures suffering and persecution. In addition, he loves Timothy. He clearly longs for Timothy to finish well.

Dietrich Bonhoeffer in his book *Life Together* rightly states, "It is not simply to be taken for granted that the Christian has the privilege of living among other Christians. Jesus Christ lived in the midst of his enemies. At the end all his disciples deserted him. On the Cross he was utterly alone, surrounded by evildoers and mockers. For this cause he had come, to bring peace to the enemies of God. So the Christian, too, belongs not in the seclusion of a cloistered life but in the thick of foes."[5] Paul's life and ministry was not unlike the Lord's. He's taking care to make sure Timothy leans into Jesus.

REFLECTION

Quite honestly, bringing Christ into our relationships is difficult sometimes. We want to offer concrete answers to life's problems. If we're not careful, our advice can seem trite—especially if we are not finding security and peace in Christ ourselves. Paul's exhortation and instruction to Timothy packs a lot more punch because he knows hardship and he clings to Christ.

Timothy Keller writes, "Jesus says, 'Follow me. I'm going to take you on a journey, and I don't want you to turn to the left or to the right. I want you to put me first; I want you to keep trusting me; to stick with me, not turn back, not give up, turn to me in all the disappointments and injustices that will happen to you. I'm going to take you places that will make you say, "Why in the world are you taking me there?" Even then, I want you to trust me.'"[6]

[5]Dietrich Bonhoeffer, *Life Together* (Harper Collins Pubishing, New York, 1954), 17.
[6]Keller 24.

Paul's first sentence says, "Paul, an apostle of Christ Jesus, by the will of God, according to the promise of life in Christ Jesus..." (II Timothy 1:1). A few verses later he reminds Timothy, and all of us, "Therefore do not be ashamed of the testimony of our Lord, or of me his prisoner, but join with me in suffering for the gospel according to the power of God, who saved us, and called us with a holy calling, not according to our works, but according to His own purpose and grace which was granted to us in Christ Jesus from all eternity" (II Timothy 1:8-9).

Unfortunately, many of us think of calling as something mysterious that happens only to a few, select people; however, the New Testament repeatedly demonstrates that all believers are called by God to follow Christ. Some are called to follow Him to another part of the world, others are called to serve Him at Starbucks, some are called to raise children. We are all called to follow Christ. Remember, as you wrote out your story in Lesson One, there was a point during the course of your life when Jesus called you to follow, and the call remains.

Remember Paul's motivation for following and suffering for the gospel was the deep love of Christ demonstrated at the cross. Does your life and do your choices reflect a growing understanding of the gospel? Why or why not?

day three

Read II Timothy

The biblical record does not give us a lot of information about Timothy, but Paul's exhortations lend insight into Timothy's background and faith, along with giving us a bird's eye view of the challenges Timothy faced. For instance we learned in Acts that Timothy was born to a Greek father and a Jewish mother. Since his father was Greek, Timothy learned the scriptures from his mother and grandmother. We also know that Paul chose him, among others, to travel with him, and that he ended up as a pastor in Ephesus. In his first letter, Paul exhorts Timothy to "let no one look down on your youthfulness" and reminds him that "by the laying on of hands" he was anointed or ordained to his role in ministry (I Timothy 4:14). In his letter to the church at Philippi, Paul says of Timothy, "I have no one else of kindred spirit...he served with me in the furtherance of the gospel like a child serving his father" (Philippians 2:19-22). These two men knew each other well.

Because of their intimate bond, Paul has earned a voice in Timothy's life. One of the first areas that Paul brings up with Timothy is similar to those he brings up in his first letter. In other words, he's not bringing up anything new. In II Timothy 1:6-7 Paul writes, "And for this reason I remind you to kindle afresh the gift of God which is in you through the laying on of my hands. For God has not given us a spirit of timidity, but of power and love and discipline." In essence Paul was exhorting Timothy, "Do not be afraid." One commentator writes, "The exhortation not to be afraid was one of the most prominent biblical assurances from God (e.g., Gen 26:24; Jer 1:8) and was a customary expression of assurance from others as well."[7]

Like all of us Timothy needed his confidence bolstered. He was young, so he needed the wisdom of an older and more experienced believer. He was afraid, so he needed courage. If you can relate, raise your hand!

---

[7]Keener, C. S., & InterVarsity Press. (1993). *The IVP Bible background commentary : New Testament* (2 Ti 1:7). Downers Grove, Ill.: InterVarsity Press.

1. What causes you to feel fearful as you follow Christ, and why?

2. According to II Timothy 1:7, with what truth did Paul seek to comfort and bolster Timothy?

3. Notably, Paul doesn't go on to reassure Timothy, "You have nothing to be afraid of in fact, everything is going to be just fine. Hang in there buddy." Quite the opposite. Look at the following and record everything Timothy had to look forward to:

II Timothy 1:8

II Timothy 2:3-6

II Timothy 3:8-12

II Timothy 4:1-5

Being a disciple of Christ involves hardship, suffering, persecution, loneliness, and misunderstanding. In fact, Jesus never promised an easy, comfortable life. He paved the way through His example, calls us to take up our cross daily, and to follow Him. Like Timothy, we will often be afraid; we will always need help; and we will need to keep in mind that we follow a risen Savior.

4. How has being a true follower of Christ been different than you imagined? In what ways has He called you to suffer for His sake—maybe in your family, or on the job, perhaps in relationships at school, or in your career? How has Jesus met you in those decisions and places of suffering and difficulty?

5. a. Compare the promise of II Timothy 1:7 with II Peter 1:2-4, and describe what you learn about the Spirit.

b. How do you draw upon the power of God's Spirit as you follow Him?

Additional Resource: *Throughout the study I will refer to www.crupressgreen.com for additional resources on various topics. If you would like to read more about the Holy Spirit and walking in the power of the Spirit, check out this link: http://crupressgreen.com/walking-in-the-spirit/*

6. Maybe you are not sure how to engage Jesus and the power of the Spirit in aspects of life outside of going to church or your small group. Based upon what you have observed so far, how might you begin to become more aware of Him and the gospel in your daily life?

REFLECTION

Thank Him for calling you to follow Him, even if you are just beginning to understand what that means. Or, if there is something hindering you from obeying his call, talk to Him about it. Consider Paul's exhortations to Timothy. Is the Lord speaking to you right now? If you are not sure, as an act of faith, tell Him that you are ready to listen and to follow His lead.

day four

Read II Timothy

Today we are going to look at a passage in Scripture that gives us a snapshot of Jesus and His disciples. This stormy collision between God and man gives us a great picture of what it is like to follow God, and it gives weight to our study of II Timothy. So, enjoy peering into the lives of Jesus and His disciples as they embark on a most memorable journey.

1. Read Matthew 8:18-22.

2. So, the scene is set. Jesus, surrounded by yet another crowd of people, orders his men to get the boat ready. They're going to the other side of the sea. Naturally a few of the guys are not ready to comply. What are the reasons they give for delaying their departure?

3.a. So, one guy is ready to follow Jesus to the ends of the earth. You would think Jesus would pat him on the back and immediately make space on the boat, but instead he paints a bleak picture. How did Jesus describe his living conditions?

b. Another disciple wanted permission to bury his father. Yet, since it does not appear he had died, it seems that this man wanted to delay his departure. How did Jesus respond?

4. Read Matthew 8:23-25 and briefly describe what happens. If you are not sure where to start, look at the following:

What did the disciples do?

Where was Jesus, and what was He doing?

What do you learn about the storm they encountered? How do the disciples feel about it?

5. I love this because it is a true picture of what it is like to follow Christ...often it means stepping out in faith into a ravaging storm. Describe a time in your life when a step of faith led to "wind and waves."

6. a. Read Matthew 8:26. It is really easy to let this scene slip by without realizing what has just happened. So, stop right here and picture the scene in your mind. Imagine being on a little boat, in the middle of an angry storm, and it is bad enough that you are convinced death is imminent. You actually have to wake Jesus up. Take careful note and describe what happens once Jesus wakes up.

b. According to Matthew 8:27, how do the disciples respond, and why?

c. How did Jesus meet you in the midst of your storm?

REFLECTION

With a word Jesus changes everything—this is what it is like to follow God. Both Paul and Timothy have seen God do incredible things in and through them. Even though Paul awaits execution, he has hope. Even though his life has been filled with suffering for the gospel, he calls his beloved son in the faith to do the same. In II Timothy 4:18 Paul writes, "The Lord will deliver me from every evil deed, and will bring me safely to His heavenly kingdom; to Him be the glory forever and ever. Amen."

How does this hope encourage you today as you step onto the boat?

Read II Timothy

Remember, Day Five questions are taken from various parts of the week's lesson. I have chosen these questions for group discussion.

1. How does the scope of redemption change your view of the gospel, or why does it matter that the story of the Bible is bigger than our experience?

2. Paul does not sugarcoat his instructions and exhortation. He is brutally honest about reality; he shares his need, his disappointments, and provides Timothy with a solid example of a man who perseveres in Christ. Why is this level of transparency so important if we are going to grow in Christ and help others to do the same?

3. Many of us think of calling as something mysterious that happens only to a few, select people; however, the New Testament repeatedly demonstrates that all believers are called by God to follow Christ. Some are called to follow Him to another part of the world; others are called to serve Him at Starbucks; some are called to raise children. We are all called to follow Christ. Remember, as you wrote out your story in Lesson One, there was a point during the course of your life when Jesus called you to follow. Think through your life's current circumstances.

a. What makes you afraid to follow Christ wholeheartedly?

b. What does it mean to know that you're called to follow Him in whatever you're involved in today?

c. How does this perspective affect your priorities?

4. a. Compare the promise of II Timothy 1:7 with II Peter 1:2-4, and describe what you learn about the Spirit.

b. How do you draw upon the power of God's Spirit as you follow Him?

5. Maybe you are not sure how to engage Jesus and the power of the Spirit in aspects of life outside of going to church or your small group. Based upon what you have observed so far, how might you begin to become more aware of Him and the gospel in your daily life?

6. After reading the story in Matthew 8:22-27, how does the insight you gained help you as you consider the fact that you are following God—the one who leads you into the storm and yet is more powerful than the wind and the seas?

LESSON THREE

Characteristics of a Disciple

Characteristics of a Disciple

One of the challenges I face personally is how to strike a balance between being disciplined and devoted to Christ without feeling like God's love and acceptance is based on my performance. What does it look like to rest in Christ and enjoy His grace while at the same time disciplining myself for the purpose of godliness? How can I continue to grow in the gospel and thrive as a disciple of Christ? Over the years I have had the privilege of meeting a handful of women, a few decades older than I, who have lived their lives with a sense of purpose and dedication, and at the same time enjoyed Jesus in a deeply personal way. These women faithfully served the Lord throughout their lives in a variety of capacities. Like all of us, they experienced a wide range of challenges, and every one of them exuded a very attractive sense of peace, trust, and faith in the Lord. Upon reflection, one thing I've learned from their example is that spiritual growth takes time. The ability to experience grace while exercising discipline and obedience is a lesson the Lord teaches us over a lifetime as we grasp more firmly the truth of the gospel.

Paul exhorts Timothy to not be ashamed, but instead to join Paul in suffering for the sake of the gospel. He reminds his son in the faith that the gospel is a treasure worth suffering for. Right in the middle of reminding Timothy of this "holy calling," he recites the gospel. He reminds Timothy that "Christ Jesus abolished death, and brought life and immortality to light through the gospel." Wow, did you catch that?

Christ Jesus abolished death.

Christ Jesus brought life through the gospel.

Christ Jesus brought immortality through the gospel.

"It is for *this reason*," Paul says, "that I suffer these things."

You see, the gospel is a serious, death-defying, life-giving, eternal message. It centers on God who became man for you and for me. Christ lived and died and rose again all because of God's rich mercy and grace. The call to live for Christ resounds. Do you hear it? As we respond to this call, we are constantly reminded of God's grace here in II Timothy and throughout Scripture. God's grace is what makes this treasure unique, worth living and dying for. J.D. Greear writes, "That's what being "gospel-centered" is really all about—not moving past the gospel, but continually going deeper into it. It's about realizing that the gospel is the final answer to every issue and problem in life and about seeing the whole world through the lens of the cross."[1]

In Lesson Two we looked at what it means to be a disciple, and this week we are going to look at the characteristics of a disciple. II Timothy 2 is full of practical exhortation and oozes the grace of God. My prayer is that our study of this chapter will provide some practical steps for following Christ and will also guide us along the path of grace as we recognize our need for Jesus and His power in every facet of life.

Pray as you begin. Ask the Lord to help your heart and soul to be open to whatever He has to teach you right now in your life.

[1]J.D. Greear, *Gospel: Recovering the Power that Made Christianity Revolutionary* (B&H Publishing, Nashville, 2011), 191.

day one

Read II Timothy

As mentioned in the introduction, there is a tension between our effort to please God and resting in His grace. Some of us feel like we have to always strive for His approval, while others of us take advantage of His grace and live however we please. Some of us care too much, and others not enough. However, we are all broken and fallen people who need His grace every day.

"You, therefore my son, be strong in the grace that is in Christ Jesus" (II Timothy 2:1). Interestingly, Paul begins this section of his letter with an exhortation to be strong in grace or *"the unmerited favor"* of God. In order to better understand what he means, we are going to employ a principle of Bible study, namely, "Let Scripture interpret Scripture."

We "let Scripture interpret Scripture" by looking to different parts of the bible that discuss the same topic we are studying to gain additional insight. In today's lesson, we are going to examine Ephesians 2:1-10, written by Paul. These ten verses describe our condition apart from Christ and then zero in on the beautiful picture of God's rich mercy and grace.

1. Read Ephesians 2:1-10.

2. Paul is writing to believers and begins with a stark reminder. According to Ephesians 2:1-3, what is true of all believers?

3. Note the contrast between II Timothy 2:1-3 and II Timothy 2:4-7. Each of these four verses reveals something about God's nature as well as His action toward us. Record what you discover:

II Timothy 2:4

II Timothy 2:5

II Timothy 2:6

II Timothy 2:7

4. According to Ephesians 2:8-9, what is true about our salvation?

5. a. Why do you think Paul begins this section by reminding us that we were dead in sin?

b. Why do you think it's imperative that we recognize God as the main subject of our salvation?

6. a. Read Ephesians 2:10 again. What is true of us and for what purpose?

b. Compare this with II Timothy 1:8-10 and 2:2. According to these verses , what is involved in being "God's workmanship"?

REFLECTION

Earlier today I chatted with a friend who repeatedly mentioned her tendency to feel guilty— guilty over not keeping her house clean, guilty because she didn't attend her son's Boy Scout award ceremony, guilty because she does not attend her church's evening service. In the same breath she explained how she was learning to experience God's grace.

Take a few minutes before you wrap up for the day. Consider Ephesians 2:1-10 in its entirety. Remind yourself that you're created in Christ Jesus for good works—by faith through God's grace. You might be like my friend and struggle with feeling guilty, like you never measure up; you are always behind when it comes to being a believer. Or you might be more carefree. Different from my friend, you might need a good strong nudge—a reminder to make time in your heart and mind for Jesus. Either way, what does it mean for you to "be strong in the grace which is in Christ Jesus"?

day two

Read II Timothy

Paul is calling Timothy to faithfully persevere for the sake of the gospel. He has reminded him of those who have deserted him and are no longer following Christ, and he exhorts Timothy to find strength in God's grace as he entrusts the gospel to faithful men and women who will do the same.

It is worth mentioning that we are studying this epistle today because Timothy and those who came after him obeyed this call.

As you read II Timothy 2:1-7, you may have noticed three different metaphors used by Paul: the soldier, the athlete, and the farmer. One of my favorite commentators, D.A. Carson, explains that these metaphors "are designed to encourage Timothy to persevere even if the task is difficult. The military metaphor shows the duty of singleness of purpose; the athletic one the need for abiding by the rules; and the agricultural one the certainty of some reward for the hard work involved. All three metaphors, drawn from everyday life, complement each other. Paul urges such reflection on this because experience would throw further light on it, as the Lord gave insight.... The following words suggest that Paul is here speaking from his own experience. The passage of nearly two thousand years has not blunted the sharpness of these everyday parallels."[2]

1. According to II Timothy 2:3-4, what are the characteristics of a "good soldier" of Christ Jesus?

---

[2]D.A. Carson, *New Bible Commentary: 21st Century Edition (4th ed.) (II Timothy 2:1-7)*, (InterVarsity Press, Downers Grove, 1994), accessed on Logos July 2013.

2. The Greek word for "entangled" is *empleko* and means "to become involved in an activity to the point of interference." Imagine you are a soldier on the front lines of battle. Like Paul mentions, your duty is to obey the orders of your commanding officer.

What would happen if you were distracted by every day details at home, and why do you think singleness of purpose is critical?

3. As disciples of Jesus, we are in an ongoing spiritual battle. In a very real sense He is our commanding officer; our goal is to please Him. However, the affairs of everyday life are very real and often very distracting.

What types of things "entangle" you, and how do these interfere with your desire to please the Lord?

A very real entanglement for me, more on an emotional level, is spending too much time dwelling on the Facebook status of my "friends." When I linger over the fun a friend is having without me, the vacation another friend is on that is way out of my price-range, or I see the success of yet another friend that rivals my own; I start to feel out of sorts. Once I begin to compare my circumstances with someone else's I'm suddenly very focused on myself, which leads me down a very unhealthy path. So, in order to un-entangle myself from that distraction I avoid visiting my Home Page. Amazingly, that has really helped me stay focused on what the Lord has for me.

4. Notice that these verses do not tell us to ignore the affairs of everyday life, but rather, to avoid being entangled by them. As you consider the things that interfere with your desire to please the Lord, what steps might you take to un-entangle yourself?

5. a. Compare II Timothy 2:5 with I Corinthians 9:24-27. What are the qualities that Paul highlights with regard to the athlete, and why do you think these are crucial for a disciple of Christ?

b. In both II Timothy and I Corinthians Paul mentions the goal or the prize. Reflect back to II Timothy 1:8-14. What is the goal for the follower of Christ, and why must we keep the goal in front of us?

6. Paul also highlights the hard working farmer. I myself have spent very little time on a farm. I find it difficult even to keep the flowers in my deck pots watered. However, I do know that if the farmer does not tend to his land, does not plant seeds at the proper time, and/or neglects to fertilize and water his crops, he yields no fruit. At the same time, there is only so much the farmer can do. Much of his time, after the crops are in, is spent waiting for growth that takes place under the earth (by the grace of our good God). Why do you think the patience of the farmer is a quality Paul includes here?

REFLECTION

The beautiful truth about Jesus Christ is that He was the perfect soldier. He never wavered from the Father's will. He was the perfect athlete—He obeyed God perfectly. He was the perfect farmer who patiently endured suffering for our sake. We are called to follow Him with focus and devotion. We are weak, but He is strong. We will fall, but He is always there to pick us up. "Be strong in the grace that is in Christ Jesus."

As you reflect on the soldier, athlete and farmer, which do you most relate to, and why?

If you were to give some attention to developing the characteristics of one of these three, which would you choose right now and why?

day three

Read II Timothy

Paul describes how to guard the treasure of the gospel and entrust it to others by using metaphors. The first three (soldier, athlete, and farmer) enable us to recognize the need to be un-entangled and focused, disciplined and devoted, and hard-working and patient. Paul continues using metaphors in the second half of this chapter. Remember, the chapter begins with a strong admonition to "be strong in grace." I firmly believe we develop in these areas over a lifetime of following the Lord, but at the same time we are a "work in progress." Each of these metaphors and the qualities highlighted are well worth our attention.

The next metaphor is the workman, and I cannot help but think of the construction crew working on a building just beyond our front deck. Over the course of just three months, we have watched as the foundation guys came and went, followed by the framers, then the roofers. Not long after the roofers finished their job, the brick-layers came, all the while the drywall guys put form to the building on the inside. And in just one week, the painters have applied two colors to the wood siding, the concrete guys poured sidewalks and landscapers planted shrubs and holly trees. None of the jobs looked easy. In fact, each required a lot of strength, skill, and diligence. If any one of the jobs had been performed poorly, it would have affected the next group's work. However, since they all did their jobs with precision, the building is nearly ready to be occupied—and in record time.

When I think of being an "unashamed workman who handles accurately the Word of truth," I picture the guys outside my window. They worked tirelessly, relentlessly, faithfully, and carefully. How much more should we, as disciples of Christ, work hard to know and share the Word of God?

1. II Timothy 2:14-19 brings God's Word to the forefront, along with the preservation of the truth. As we will see in chapter three, false teachers are ever present. In this section of the letter, Paul uses the metaphor of the "unashamed workman" to explain to Timothy how he should present himself to God.

a. According to II Timothy 2:14-19, what is the main task of the workman?

b. In II Timothy 2:14, 16-17, Paul draws a stark contrast between the workman who is approved of God and those who are useless. What type of people does Paul exhort Timothy to avoid and why?

The Scripture is full of passages advising us to use our words carefully, and there are numerous passages that warn us to beware of false teachers. This particular passage exhorts us to learn how to handle the Word of God accurately, which takes diligence and time. What I love about the Bible is that God has made it simple enough for a child to understand and complex enough to keep even the most scholarly students of Scripture on their knees. What I hope we will all gain from this passage is a deeper appreciation for God's truth and our need to continually grow in our ability to understand the Word. For some of us this simply means we need to keep reading it. For others it might mean diving in a little deeper, buying a commentary or two, and making a more concerted effort. Still others might sense the need to get more education. No matter what, as we follow the Lord, spending time in the riches of His Word and growing in our understanding of His Word is essential to spiritual growth.

2. What are ways you are growing in your appreciation for the truth of God's Word, and how can you continue to deepen your understanding of Scripture?

3. According to II Timothy 2:19, what is the "firm foundation of God" and why, in the context of what we have been studying, does Paul include this?

4. Abstaining from wickedness is a clear command of Scripture and ties into the fifth metaphor—the vessel of honor.

   a. What are the characteristics of the honorable vessel (II Timothy 2:21)?

   b. Read II Timothy 2:20-23. From what are we to flee and why?

   c. How can you apply this exhortation to your life today? Consider from what do you need to flee or what must you pursue.

5. a. What are the qualities of the sixth metaphor—the Lord's servant (II Timothy 2:24-26), and what is God's role in the life of the servant?

b. Reflect back to Ephesians 2:1-10 (Day One), and the rich mercy of God. Compare Ephesians 2:10 with II Timothy 2:24-26. What insights or encouragement to you gain?

6. a. Reflect on the metaphors of the workman, vessel, and servant. Why do you think Paul uses these particular examples?

b. Which metaphor and corresponding exhortation is most applicable to your life right now and why?

REFLECTION

If you were to zero in on one or two areas of your life that need some attention (keep in mind the six metaphors in our passage), which would you choose and why?

day four

Read II Timothy

As we wrap up our look at the soldier, athlete, farmer, workman, vessel, and servant, I could not help but notice the specific and particular instructions Paul gives to Timothy. This section of Paul's letter cannot be read without sensing a need to take some sort of action, don't you agree? Of course that action will look different depending upon our circumstances and place in life.

So, I want to give you an opportunity to create a "Personal Development Plan" (PDP). The purpose for this plan is to help you focus on a few areas of your life in such a way that will help you in your pursuit of Christ as His disciple. Before we look at the Personal Development Plan, take a look back to II Timothy 2:7-13. Paul reminds Timothy to rely on the Lord.

1. What promise does Paul encourage Timothy with in II Timothy 2:7?

2. a. Notice that Paul interjects the gospel in II Timothy 2:7-8. What does he highlight in these verses?

b. What is Paul's motivation—his personal mission statement if you will—according to II Timothy 2:9-10?

3. Carefully consider the "trustworthy statement" (which is most likely a hymn) which looks beyond the present sufferings to our future glory. Here the disciple of Christ finds great assurance because dying and living (2:11) represent the believer's identification with Christ's death and resurrection (see also Romans 6:1-11).

As we persevere through the challenges of this present life, we can also rest assured that we will one day reign with Him in glory. Additionally, there is a sober warning for those who deny Christ—He will also deny them.

This hymn ends on a reassuring note for those who are faithless—He remains faithful. How encouraging is that? No matter how often our faith falters, He is God. He cannot deny Himself. Why is this reassuring?

4. Now we are going to utilize the Personal Development Plan. I have used something like the following plan over the course of my adult life and have found it to be quite helpful. For one thing, it forces me to stop and take a breath. It helps me stop and listen for the Lord's voice. Sometimes I involve myself in activities that I think are a good idea, but I have not really prayed for wisdom or guidance. Sometimes by taking the time to consider my circumstances, this plan will help me get back on course. On numerous occasions, the Lord has used it to surface areas of my life that I was neglecting.

The purpose of this development plan is to help you consider the areas in which the Lord is nudging you to think more deeply about as His follower. I include it here so that you can look back over II Timothy 1-2 and ask the Lord to help you to grow in grace and the knowledge of Him.

a. Reflect back over this lesson—you have already done some work that will help you with this exercise. Remember Ephesians 2:10 and II Timothy 2:2. You are God's workmanship, created in Christ Jesus for good works, which God prepared beforehand that you should walk in them. Pray He will guide you on the path He has laid out for you.

b. Think about the admonitions surrounding the soldier, athlete, farmer, workman, vessel, and servant. Go back over the questions you answered for Days 1-3. Here are a few to get you started:

Are there areas in your daily life that tend to entangle and distract you?

Is there recurring sin that the Lord reminded you about as you studied—like jealousy, greed, lust, anger—that continues to pop up in your heart and keep you from intimacy with the Lord and others? If so, what is the root of that sin? Fear of failure? An unhealthy need to be accepted? How might focusing on that particular area of your life help you grow?

Do you lack discipline? Do you find yourself saying, "I try to spend time with Jesus but I always get sidetracked. I really want to grow but I just never have time?

c. Consider the message of the gospel as you work through your plan. We talk often about "preaching the gospel to ourselves and each other." How can the gospel encourage you as you seek to grow in Christ?

Add other good questions that you can ask yourself, or talk to a close friend. Use the questions on the PDP to prompt your thinking. But, mostly try to go back over what the Lord has shown you in the study to help inform your plan.

PERSONAL DEVELOPMENT PLAN

Name:_____ Discipler:_____

Need: My areas where I see a need for growth:	*Goal:* I will know I have grown in this area when...(it helps if your answer is "achievable and measureable").	*Root Issues:* What are the root issues that hinder my growth? Why is this a need in my life?	*Resources:* What are some of the steps I can take to help me develop in this? Other resources (like books or videos) I can access?	*Next Steps:* What do I need to learn? What resources do I need? What will I do? When will I do it?

day five

Read II Timothy

The women I mentioned in the introduction to this week's lesson all had a sense of purpose for their lives. One of my older friends was Dorothy who died just after her 87th birthday. Although she was limited physically, she never stopped seeking the Lord. She was an example of an "approved workman who handled accurately the word of truth." My friend Shirley is 76 years old and travels to and from Russia as a missionary. I receive her ministry newsletter, and she always talks about what she is learning from the Lord and includes pictures of women with whom she is entrusting the treasure of the gospel. Muriel is 82 and continues to walk by faith as the Lord uses her to mentor younger women through her writing and her counseling ministry at Multnomah Bible College and Seminary. I am so thankful for these women, and their examples spur me on. I hope this lesson and your Personal Development Plan encourages you to excel still more—in the grace that is in Christ Jesus.

These questions are taken from this week's lesson and should be helpful as you fill out your Personal Development Plan. Discuss your plan with your group and ask for accountability where appropriate.

1. The Greek word for "entangled" is *empleko* and means "to become involved in an activity to the point of interference." What types of things "entangle" you, and how does these interfere with your walk with the Lord?

2. As you reflect on the soldier, athlete and farmer, workman, vessel, and servant which do you most relate to, and why?

3. If you were to give some attention to developing the characteristics of one of these three, which would you choose right now and why?

4. Paul's mission statement almost vibrates off the page in 2:9-10. How might we cultivate the same intensity for the gospel?

5. If you were to zero in on one or two areas of your life that need some attention (keep in mind the six metaphors in our passage), which would you choose and why?

6. Pray for each other as you work on this project.

LESSON FOUR

Beware!

Beware!

Does it make any difference how our culture is defined or described? As believers in Jesus Christ, do we need to be aware of the affects of the trends in society?

Over the past several years as I've engaged in spiritual conversations with people from all walks of life, I've realized more and more that a lot of people have no idea who Jesus is. Or if they do, it is often a caricature of someone they learned about in Sunday school but not necessarily accurate to the Biblical record. On the one hand, I run into many who have never dawned the doors of a church, and on the other, I meet many who attended church as a child but have chosen not to continue pursuing God or religion because of a bad experience.

An increasing sense of religious apathy and pervasive unbelief has surfaced in America, which some say is the result of "postmodern" thinking. Millard Erikson, in his book *The Postmodern World: Discerning the Times and the Spirit of Our Age*, states, "There are no universal values, which apply everywhere for everyone. Nor are right and wrong different for each individual. Rather, each group sets its own standards, which are valued and normative...attempting to persuade someone to your point of view shows disrespect."[1] The sense of apathy and unbelief continues to increase even though natural disasters and economic chaos continue to strike our country. This is a time of great opportunity for the gospel and for discipleship.

We are taking steps, as the body of Christ, to become much more aware of the needs around us, and believers are beginning to purposefully penetrate the society on a variety of levels. We also must be aware of the culture around us so that we do not succumb to faulty thinking. George Barna's statistics reveal that only 49 percent of born again Christians believe that moral truth is absolute, which reflects the postmodern influence mentioned earlier. This kind of thinking is having a huge impact on the church today.

---

[1] Millard Erikson, *The Postmodern World: Discerning the Times and the Spirit of Our Age* (Wheaton, Ill.: Crossway Books, 2002), 14,17.

Some 2000 years ago, Paul exhorted Timothy, "In the last days difficult times will come." We live in the last days, too, and I think we are all aware that difficult times are here. Remember that this exhortation comes on the heels of the call to live with the various qualities of a soldier, athlete, farmer, workman, vessel, and bondservant. Adhering to the call of God, holding fast to His truth, and living in such a way that draws people to Christ lays the groundwork for this week's lesson.

As you begin this week's lesson, pray for wisdom and a heightened sensitivity to the Lord and His Word.

day one

Read II Timothy

1. Discuss ways have you noticed, felt or encountered the effects of a religiously stagnant society. Why do you think it is important that we are aware of the shifts in our culture?

2. Paul is concerned for Timothy and wants to leave him well-prepared for the battle before him. He encourages him to stir up the gift of God and to stand firm in God's power, love, and discipline. He urges him to stand firm in God's grace and reminded him of the Lord's enduring faithfulness. Ultimately, Paul reminds Timothy that he suffers, perseveres and endures for the sake of God's treasure—the gospel. Now he focuses on the effects of the culture around him.

a. Look at II Timothy 3:1-9. Make a list of the characteristics that describe the "last days".

b. Take each characteristic and write down ways you see these evidenced in your daily life, perhaps in commercials, popular books, or trends, as you engage in conversation with people at work, etc.

3. In II Timothy 3:5, Paul tells Timothy to avoid false teachers who preach anything contrary to the gospel. Compare this passage with the following, and record additional insight you gain regarding false teaching.

Romans 16:17-19

II Thessalonians 3:6

Jude 17-21

4. According to II Timothy 3:6-7, what kind of people tend to fall prey to lies?

Notably Paul is warning Timothy against the false teachers of his day. He describes them as men who appear to be godly but in actuality have nothing to do with Jesus Christ. Peter warns of this same danger in II Peter 2 where he describes false teachers as those who "secretly introduce destructive heresies, even denying the Master who bought them" (II Peter 2:1). He describes these heretics as greedy, indulgent, despisers of authority, daring and self-willed.

In today's passage Paul refers to Jannes and Jambres (they were magicians who opposed Moses whose reputations the readers of this letter were most likely familiar with from Exodus 7:1-24). Commentators Beale and Carson explain, "They [Jannes and Jambres] came to represent Moses' arch nemeses who would counter his displays of divine power with various tricks of their own; and by their association with various stories...they acquired symbolic status as opponents of the truth."[2]

Opposition to the truth of God and the gospel has existed from the beginning of time, and just as Paul warned Timothy some 2000 years ago, we need to heed the same warning today.

REFLECTION

Recently, while facilitating a discussion on a passage in the New Testament, one of the most extroverted guys in the group explained that he viewed the Bible as an "ancient book having no relevance to his life today." He attended church, wanted to be involved in Christian things, and yet, the Bible had no bearing on his life or decisions. He is a great example of today's culture, and he reflects where many people stand when it comes to the authority of the Bible.

Are there ways in which your view of truth has been influenced by today's culture? Explain.

In light of today's study, why do you think it is important to view the Bible as God's truth, and how would you describe your view of the Bible at this point in your walk with God?

---

[2]G.K. Beale, D.A. Carson, *Commentary on the New Testament Use of the Old Testament* (Baker Academic, Grand Rapids, 2007), 907.

day two

Read II Timothy

As we have marched our way through this very personal letter, it is important to note that Paul is very explicit in his instructions to Timothy. He does not mince words, nor does he make suggestions with a question mark at the end. "Um, Tim, I was just thinking that if you were to think about stirring up that little gift from God...I mean, if you have time...you might experience some of that divine power, love and discipline we talked about over coffee the other day."

He does not give him options. "Tim, buddy, sometimes being like a solider is a good idea—gets you off the couch I've heard. Oh, and some say it is good to watch the Olympics—it might be a way to harness some inspiration. You might want to think about getting into spiritual shape...it is up to you."

Paul is not middle of the road: "Try and avoid youthful lusts Timmy. You know they're not good for you. I know it is hard sometimes—everything is so tempting and attractive especially when you are trying to serve the Lord."

Quite the contrary!

Do not be ashamed.
Retrain the standard of sound words.
Guard the treasure.
Stand firm in grace.
Suffer hardship.
Be diligent.
Avoid worldly and empty chatter.
Remember Jesus Christ risen from the dead.
Flee youthful lusts.
Refuse foolish and ignorant speculation.
Avoid such men as these.

As we continue on in chapter three, Paul continues to be quite explicit in his instruction. I have mentioned this before, but following Christ is a serious calling for every child of God. Thank the Lord for calling you to be His child. Thank Him for His grace and His truth, and pray He'll use both to give you understanding as you study today.

1.a. In very honest terms, what attracts you to the world and consequently distracts you from following Christ?

b. In what ways does Paul allude to some of those same things as he encourages Timothy, and why do you think it is important that we are honest with our struggles and shortcomings?

2. As you read II Timothy 3:10-17 notice that Paul shifts subjects. He directly addresses Timothy. What are his specific exhortations?

II Timothy 3:10-11

II Timothy 3:14-15

3. a. What is true of those who desire to live godly in Christ Jesus compared with evil men and imposters? How was this evident in Paul's life according to these verses?

b. In what ways do you face opposition as you seek to live godly in Christ Jesus? Perhaps your choices affect the way you do your job, or the way you engage in relationships. How do people interact with you as a result of your way of life?

4. a. Look again at II Timothy 3:14-17. What are the different ways Scripture is used in Timothy's life?

b. In these same verses Paul describes various truths about Scripture. List them here.

5. Paul reminds Timothy that Scripture causes the man or woman of God to be "adequate, equipped for every good work." How have you seen this to be true in your life? Or, if you are new to the Word, how might you turn to God's Word to help you in your circumstances today?

LESSON FOUR: BEWARE! 79

REFLECTION

Describe a point in time when the Lord used Scripture in a profitable way in your life. Consider questions like: What was your need, and what drew you to the Word? How did you respond? What difference did it make in your life?

As you consider the opposition you face as a believer, how has God used His Word to give you strength, wisdom or encouragement?

Describe one or two ways you can use the Bible to guide you today.

day three

Read II Timothy

In light of the relativistic culture in which we live, it is important that we seek to grasp the authority of Scripture. While this will no means be an exhaustive look at the subject, my prayer is that it will help us stand with confidence on the truth of God's Word and at least know where to begin if and when we engage with men and women who question the validity and authority of the Bible.

John Stott in his bible study *II Timothy-Standing in Truth* states, "The two reasons Timothy should remain loyal to what he had come firmly to believe were that he had learned it from Old Testament Scripture and from the apostle Paul. The same two grounds apply today. The gospel we believe is the biblical gospel, the gospel of the Old Testament and the New Testament, vouched for by both the prophets of God and the apostles of Christ."[3]

1. Look, once again, at II Timothy 3:15-17. What is the origin of God's Word?

"The word *inspired* comes from the Greek word *theopneustos* which means "god-breathed." *Theos* is the Greek word for God, and *pneustos* is from the word *pneuma*, which means "air," "wind," or "breath." The combination of the two Greek words means "God-breathed." God breathed in (and out) of the sacred writers of Scripture what He wanted them to write, and thus it was God's Word, complete and without error.... Thus we see that God has "breathed" the Scriptures through us with the result that all Scripture is profitable for us in a practical, day-to-day application."[4]

[3]John Stott, *II Timothy-Stand in Truth* (Intervarsity Press, Downers Grove, 1998), 41.
[4]James T. Draper, Kenneth Keathley, *Biblical Authority: The Critical Issue for the Body of Christ* (Broadman & Holleman, Nashville, 2001), 79.

2. Compare this with the following verses and record what you learn about God's Word:

Hebrews 4:12

I Peter 1:23-25

II Peter 1:20-21

3. All throughout His ministry, Jesus referred to and rested in the truth of Scripture. Take a look at Luke 24:13-27. How did Jesus go about explaining the crucifixion and resurrection?

All throughout the Old Testament the prophets continually spoke the Word of God. They were His mouthpiece for the nation of Israel. From Moses all the way to the New Testament, these words were written down and preserved by the nation of Israel. We are fortunate to see the whole drama of redemption right in our laps or on our phones!

4. Jesus also explains the role of the Holy Spirit with regard to the Scripture in John 16:12-14.

a. Read these verses and record what they reveal about the Spirit and the Word.

b. How does this passage encourage you in your quest to know the Word?

REFLECTION

Volumes of information have been written on the topic of Biblical Authority and Inspiration, and in this short lesson, we have barely scratched the surface. What is important is that we continue to grow in our understanding of God's Word. When our beliefs are challenged, or our conduct is ridiculed, or when we lose heart and wonder what our purpose is, we need to lean into Jesus and dig into His Word. My confidence in the validity of Scripture is enhanced when I measure it against the character of God and the resurrected Christ. My personal experience attests to the fact that God uses His Word to teach us, to mold and shape us. It really is living and active and definitely profitable.

As you finish up, read Psalm 19 and consider all the different ways the Lord uses His Word to refresh our lives. Make Psalm 19:7-14 your prayer.

day four

Read II Timothy

Society today does not lend itself to quiet contemplation or reflective reading. We are in a hurry to accomplish the next task or get ahead of the next trend. We seek depth of meaning in 140 characters or less and often communicate our most difficult circumstances by texting.

So, I would not find it surprising if reading II Timothy over and over again has proven frustrating at times. The words feel very familiar and almost boring by now, right? What is the point of reading the book yet again? Eugene Peterson, author of *Eat This Book,* says, "Reading is an immense gift, but only if the words are assimilated, taken into the soul—eaten, chewed, gnawed, received in unhurried delight...The danger in all reading is that words be twisted into propaganda or reduced to information, mere tools and data. We silence the living voice and reduce words to what we can use for convenience and profit."[5] Peterson urges us to read spiritually, which means "participating in our reading, receiving the words in such a way that they become interior to our lives, the rhythms and images becoming practices of prayer, acts of obedience, ways of love."[6] Not only will this participatory approach to God's Word change us, it might drastically change the way we look at the lost world around us.

Remember, we are called to handle the word of truth with skill and accuracy (II Timothy 2:15) as we stand on the front lines of the last days. Since truth is relative in our culture, it is all the more important that we grow in our understanding of God and His Word— together. Gabe Lyons in his book, *The Next Christians: How A New Generation is Restoring the Faith,* describes how spiritually vibrant believers in today's culture "have rediscovered Scripture and immerse themselves in it in a way that differs from the practice of recent generations...they aren't determined to find verses to support their opinions or point of view. Instead, they enjoy Scripture as they believe it was meant to be: a grand narrative

---

[5]Peterson, 11.
[6]Peterson, 10.

that tells a story of a God who loves and pursues, rescues, gives grace, and goes to any length to restore relationships with his most prized creations."[7]

1. As you consider discipleship—both being discipled and discipling others, do you find it natural or difficult to bring Scripture into conversations? Why?

2. How might your relationships change if the Word was more a part of your interaction?

3. Both Eugene Peterson and Gabe Lyons talk about engaging with the Scripture, entering into the drama of the whole story. How is this different than your usual approach to the Word?

4. As you consider the authority of the Bible, which we looked at in Lesson Three, what is lost if we don't look to and apply it to our lives and relationships? What is gained when we do?

---

[7]Gabe Lyons, *The Next Christians: How A New Generation is Restoring the Faith* (Doubleday, New York, 2010), 135.

REFLECTION

Look, once again, at Psalm 19 (we ended Lesson Three in this Psalm).

Incredibly, the Psalmist describes how the heavens speak of the glory of God and remind us all day long—never uttering an audible word—that God is here, everywhere around us. I find comfort knowing God is always with me, don't you? As you reflect on Psalm 19:7-11, under what circumstances does the writer look to the Word?

Our needs are just like those he lists—we need restoration, comfort, wisdom, and warning. Take some time on your own, and then in your group, and talk about how the Word can and does reach into to the very heart of life's challenges.

Talk to at least one of your friends, or someone you disciple, this week, and take a step and open up the Word together. Share about the things you are learning from II Timothy and this study.

day five

Remember, these questions are taken from the previous four days and will be discussed in your group this week.

1. Discuss ways have you noticed, felt or encountered the effects of today's culture. Why do you think it is important that we are aware of the way most people look at God and religion today?

2. Are there ways in which your view of truth has been influenced by the postmodern culture? Explain.

3. Why do you think it is important to view the Bible as God's truth?

4. As you have opportunity to encourage other believers in the faith, or as you engage with unbelievers, how can you make sure that your beliefs and convictions are rooted and grounded in truth?

5. What did the following verses teach you about God's Word?

Hebrews 4:12

I Peter 1:23-25

II Peter 1:20-21

6. As you consider discipleship – both being discipled and discipling others, do you find it natural or difficult to bring Scripture into conversations? Why?

7. As you consider the authority of the Bible, which we looked at in Lesson Three, what is lost if we don't look to and apply it to our lives and relationships? What is gained when we do?

LESSON FIVE

Be Ready!

Be Ready!

In the first lesson of our study, I included this quote from *The True Story of the Whole World* where the authors explain that the real-life drama of redemptive history "begins with God's creation of the universe and human rebellion and runs through the history of Israel to Jesus and on through the Church, moving to the coming kingdom of God. At the very center of this story is the man called Jesus of Nazareth, in whom God has revealed his fullest purpose and meaning for the world. Only this one story unlocks the meaning of human history—and thus the meaning of your life and mine."[1] Hopefully, after spending time in II Timothy, God's purpose and meaning for the world, and for your own life, is clearer than when we first began.

Certainly Timothy's circumstances were very different than ours, but the call to guard the treasure of the gospel, to entrust it to faithful men and women, to persevere despite opposition rings loud and true for every believer. The next generation depends upon our obedient response to the call. This week we are going to reflect back over the past four lessons and II Timothy 1-3, along with our personal experience and musings, to help inform our next steps. This will not be an exhaustive look at discipleship, by any means, but I hope it will help you engage in the lives of people in your sphere of influence.

Also, just in case there is come confusion between the word "mentor" and "mentoree" and "discipler" and "disciple", I have chosen to use the forms of the word disciple because it is most consistent with the New Testament.

What is a disciple?

The word disciple, or *mathetes* in the original Greek, means "the pupil or apprentice of a teacher." It is used over 260 times in the New Testament.

"Although Jesus (like John) was not an officially recognized teacher (Jn. 7:14f.), he was popularly known as a teacher or rabbi (Mk. 9:5; 11:21; Jn. 3:2), and his associates were

---

[1]Craig Bartholomew, Michael Goheen, *The True Story of the Whole World: Finding Your Place in the Biblical Drama* (Faith Alive Christian Resources, Grand Rapids, 2004), 12.

known as disciples. [Discipleship] involved personal allegiance to him, expressed in following him and giving him an exclusive loyalty (Mk. 8:34–38; Lk. 14:26–33). In at least some cases it meant literal abandonment of home, business ties and possessions (Mk. 10:21, 28), but in every case readiness to put the claims of Jesus first, whatever the cost, was demanded."[2]

[2]BIBLIOGRAPHY. K. H. Rengstorf, TDNT 4, pp. 415–460; E. Schweizer, *Lordship and Discipleship*, 1960; M. Hengel, *Nachfolge und Charisma*, Berlin, 1968; *NIDNTT* 1, pp. 480–494.

day one

Read II Timothy

Remember, you are part of the true story of the whole world. Bartholomew and Goheen describe the resurrection of Jesus Christ as "the explosive event that prompts change" in our lives.[1] Before he ascended into heaven, Jesus proclaimed, "All authority in heaven and on earth has been given to Me. Go, therefore, and make disciples of all nations, baptizing them in the name of the Father, the Son, and the Holy Spirit, teaching them to observe all that I commanded you; and lo, I am with you always, even to the end of the earth" (Matthew 28:18-20). The call to "make disciples" is not optional, a "take it or leave it" kind of choice. We are all called to make disciples.

1. a. As you contemplate what we have studied so far regarding what it means to be a disciple of Christ, describe someone who is presently in your life and is actively following Jesus. Why did you choose this person?

b. How do you know he/she follows Jesus? For example, how does he/she make decisions? What drives his/her satisfaction and security?

c. What both appeals to, and challenges you, about this person's life of faith?

[1] Bartholomew and Goheen, 148.

Paul was Timothy's consistent model—he exemplified a life wholly devoted to Jesus Christ. We have seen that Paul spent *time* with Timothy. They traveled together, preached the gospel together, labored over ministry challenges together. In addition, Paul spent a good deal of time *teaching* Timothy the meaning of the gospel, truth about Jesus, how to lead a church, etc. Through both word and deed Paul taught Timothy what it meant to be a follower of Christ. Paul also showed a great amount of *tenderness* toward his son in the faith. He knew Timothy's points of weakness and vulnerability, always encouraged and believed in him, and did everything he could—even on his deathbed—to make sure Timothy was prepared for the long haul of following the Savior. Take a few minutes and think about the people who have demonstrated time, teaching, and tenderness toward you.

2. What kind of time did these people spend with you, and what difference did their time make?

3. Record some of the most meaningful things these individuals taught you, and how does their teaching impact your walk with the Lord today?

4. In what ways did you experience tenderness in these relationships, and why was their tenderness significant?

In a few of our previous lessons, I mentioned different women who have impacted my life in deep and lasting ways. Some I had the privilege of spending time with over the course of several years. Others I would see only periodically, but in either case, I can still recall and often repeat the truths they taught me either directly through the Word or indirectly through their time and tenderness.

REFLECT

Take a few minutes today and write a note of thanks, or send an email or text, to the person (or people) who discipled you by encouraging you to walk with Jesus. Say thank you for their time, teaching and tenderness.

day two

Read II Timothy

In my experience I have come to realize that there are a variety of ways that discipleship actually happens. The following descriptions are brief and definitely not exhaustive. What I hope to do by including them is to demonstrate a variety of ways in which we can be involved in discipleship with people already in our lives; or how often, the relationships right under our noses are meant to take on more depth. We simply need to step out in faith.

Sometimes you might begin a relationship with an unbeliever. As the relationship grows, often over the course of time, the Lord opens the door for the gospel to be shared, and your friend comes to know Christ as Savior. The next natural step (as outlined in Matthew 28:18-20) is to encourage baptism, and then to help this person grow in his or her understanding of Jesus Christ through the Bible. My family moved into a new neighborhood when I was a senior in high school. Our neighbor, Lynn, formed a relationship with my mom and me (I often babysat for her). Over the course of a few years she shared the gospel with us. She lived for Jesus and she talked about Him all of the time. Eventually, when I hit a crisis in my life, she explained to me how to receive Christ, which I did. A year later so did my mom, and eventually almost our whole family started walking with the Lord! She did not stop there. She continued to teach us how to read the Word, how to pray, how to live for Him. Lynn was a stay-at-home-mom who made disciples everywhere she went.

Or you might lead a small group through your church, and through this group you could easily meet someone who is eager to grow. Your role would include spending regular time with this person—inviting her into different aspects of your own life: helping her move into a new home, helping her make decisions about the future, or encouraging her through a difficult time. You could pray with and for her. Sometimes this type of relationship grows into a lifelong friendship. Some of my closest friends today are women who were in small groups I led when I was in college.

I have found, the older I get, that I often spend snippets of time with younger women. It seems I'm sought out more often for counsel in certain situations, and I tend to have more relationships with younger women that are less time-intensive, but often involve more serious issues than when I was younger. It requires availability on my part in a whole different way.

I also firmly believe that we all disciple one another through our friendships. Just because I have walked with the Lord for a long time does not mean that I do not need spiritual encouragement. I deeply value the friendships I have with women who talk with me about Jesus and encourage me from His Word. For some reason we sometimes fail to see the relationship right in front of us as one that can point us to a rich walk with Christ.

1. So, as you consider your life, think through the various types of discipleship relationships I have described. Describe relationships where you see yourself being a disciple—receiving input and truth, encouragement and care from another believer; and, relationships where you see yourself providing input and truth, encouragement and care for another (perhaps younger) believer. List both those that are either happening or are possible in your life today.

2. a. If you listed potential discipleship relationships, what keeps you from being more intentional in your friendship or relationship? You might list things like fear, lack of time, etc.

b. Scan II Timothy. How does this letter address each of your hesitations?

3. How could you spend a little more time with this person, and if you did, how could you be intentional about your conversation?

I have learned that often I have to take the initiative, whether I want to spend time with someone who might need help and encouragement or if I want to get to know someone in order to learn from her. Sometimes the time I spend is by texting. A dear friend of mine is a busy mom. The majority of our deeper conversations are spent over texting and email. Even though we do not connect regularly face to face, we stay in close touch with each other. We pray for each other—in the moment— because we text. Another young woman, a student at a college many miles from where I live, will often text me when things reach a crisis point in her life. I pray for her, I send her Scripture, and I counsel her. Once the crisis fades, I do not hear from her as often. Interestingly, I met her because we both have fibromyalgia, and her sister thought I might be able to encourage her. We connected first through email and have remained in touch for almost ten years. I have never met her in person! Discipleship takes on many different forms in the 21st Century.

4. List two or three of the truths you have learned from II Timothy that are foundational for believers—whether young or old in Christ—and why? As you think about the person (or persons) you listed in question #1, what have you learned that you can impart to her/him/them?

5. Tenderness does not always come easily for me. I have had to learn compassion the hard way and have chosen over the years to share more vulnerably about my own struggles. I find that the more authentic I am about my questions, difficulties, fears and failings, the more freedom others have to share theirs with me. How would showing tenderness toward the person you are discipling make a difference in your relationship?

REFLECTION

I can imagine that there is some aspect of discipleship that is challenging at this point. Maybe you feel pressed by time. Perhaps you do not see possibilities for discipleship in your present or future circumstances. It could be that like Timothy, you feel timid or insecure. Maybe you have had a bad experience and you are hesitant, or you simply do not feel equipped. Tell the Lord how you are feeling, and if you are willing to step out in faith and make yourself available...express your fears and your faith to Jesus.

day three

Read II Timothy

Before we look at some particular aspects of discipleship, I want to look once again at the Bible and discover a little more about the discipleship relationship. Of course our greatest teacher, and the One to whom we look, is Jesus. While His time on earth was quite short, the time He spent with the disciples was intense. In addition, we can learn from other relationships Paul had by looking at a few of the other letters he wrote.

1. Read Matthew 4:12-25. Jesus is just beginning His public ministry. He has just come from the wilderness where He faced the temptation of the devil, and He begins to proclaim that the kingdom of heaven is at hand.

a. According to Matthew 4:18-22, whom does Jesus encounter and to what were they invited?

b. What words does Matthew chose to describe these men's response?

2. Continue reading Matthew 4:23-25. Record the events that took place between Jesus, Peter, Andrew, James and John.

Read Matthew 5:1-7:27. This section of Matthew is called "The Sermon on the Mount," and Jesus is proclaiming the news of God's kingdom. As you read, put yourself in the shoes of the disciples. Not long before they were minding their own business, mending nets and tending to their daily catch of fish. Suddenly, Jesus intersects their lives and calls them to follow. As He spent time with them, He taught them the ways of God's kingdom. He explained the source of true happiness, taught them how to pray, explained how to deal with an enemy and pointed to the true source of provision and treasure. All along He showed mercy and compassion for the sick and needy.

3. According to Matthew 7:28-29, how did the crowd view Jesus and His teaching? We have the benefit of knowing the end of the story for these men who were once fisherman. But what can we learn from Jesus about discipleship?

4. Skip over to Matthew 8:14-27. I often wonder how much time passed between the day Jesus called Peter to follow—the day Peter dropped everything and left—to this moment when Jesus is in Peter's home healing his mother-in-law. What insight do you gain about Jesus' ministry, including time, teaching and tenderness?

The chapters we have looked at today precede Jesus calming the wind and the sea, which we looked at in an earlier lesson. I am reminded that following Jesus is at once an amazing adventure and also a letting go—a surrendering of—our best-laid plans. He gets into the most personal side of our lives and leads us to places we never dreamed of. One of those places is the call to build the gospel into the heart and life of another person.

REFLECTION

I include another rather broad overview of discipleship today to remind you that the New Testament is full of examples of relationships like the one we have been studying. Jesus is our perfect model, and no matter how "over our heads" we feel or how inadequate or unprepared we may be, the Lord gives us instruction through His Word, power through His Spirit and grace in the gospel. Thank Him for each of these truths today.

day four

Read II Timothy

We have covered a lot of ground this week! I hope you have been encouraged both by the way the Lord has provided people to help you grow and the ways He is providing people for you to pour into. Today we are going to peruse a ministry site that provides all kinds of great tools for discipleship and small groups. All you will need for today is your computer. You might be tempted to skip over this lesson, or to put it off until another day, but take the time to look at the resources available.

1. Make a discipleship file on your computer, in Evernote, Dropbox or wherever you store information.

2. My favorite site, probably because I'm most familiar with the tools, is *CruPressGreen:*

crupressgreen.com/category/resources/personal-discipleship/basic-growth-concepts/

3. If you visit *Resources* and then *Basic Growth Concepts* you will find both written and video tutorials.

The simplest material to use with a new believer is found on Page One: *Basic Follow-up Classic Version*. It includes four short studies that walk a new believer through *How To Be Sure You're A Christian, Assurance of Salvation, The Ministry of the Holy Spirit, How to Grow.*

You might also enjoy *Conducting Basic Follow-up/Postcards From Corinth.* This provides excellent teaching for a new believer and is more comprehensive than the *Follow-up Classic Version.*

The Transferable Concepts is also a great series for a new believer or for a small group with new believers.

Click through all three pages to get a feel for what is available.

Download either *Follow-up Classic Version* or *Conducting Basic Follow-up/Postcards from Corinth*, and anything else you find helpful, and save it to your file.

4. If you are sharing the gospel with someone, click on the Evangelism tab, and then Evangelism Training and you will find a variety of tools to help you share the gospel in various situations. Again, click through all three pages to see what is available.

Now, visit ***www.startingwithgod.com*** and download *"Email Series, How To Talk About God"* to your file. Add anything else you find helpful to your file.

5. If you use an iPhone, iPad, or Smartphone download the **GodTools** app and have basic resources available with you wherever you go.

REFLECTION

After perusing these different resources, what is one step you will take in discipleship as a result of what you have seen?

Read II Timothy

These questions are taken from the previous four days and are designed to generate group discussion.

1. a. As you contemplate what we have studied so far regarding what it means to be a disciple of Christ, describe someone who is presently in your life and is actively following Jesus. What characterizes this person's life such as decision-making, holding down a career or nurturing a marriage/family?

b. How do you know he/she follows Jesus? For example, how does he/she make decisions? What drives his/her satisfaction and security?

c. What both appeals to you and challenges you about this person's life of faith?

2. So, as you consider your life, think through the various types of discipleship relationships I have described. Describe relationships where you see yourself being a disciple—receiving input and truth, encouragement and care from another believer, and describe relationships where you see yourself providing input and truth, encouragement and care for another (perhaps younger) believer. List both those that are either happening or are possible in your life today.

3. a. If you listed potential discipleship relationships, what keeps you from being more intentional in your friendship or relationship? You might list things like fear, lack of time, etc.

b. Scan II Timothy. How does this letter address each of your hesitations?

4. What is one step you will take in discipleship as a result of what you found online?

LESSON SIX

Fix Your Eyes on the Prize

Fix Your Eyes on the Prize

I met Marion McIlhaney not long after Bob and I moved to Austin, Texas. We'd been married for three years, and our move to Texas was the beginning of a life of adventure as we followed Christ together. Not long after we settled in, I began attending a women's bible study at our church of which Marion was the teacher. She was on the verge of turning 50, had three grown daughters, taught the bible with passion, and shared openly and honestly about a variety of challenges she was facing. I loved listening to her teach and deeply admired her walk with the Lord. Soon after that first gathering, I invited her to lunch and asked her if she would disciple me. She was surprised by my question, and asked, "What would that look like?" I responded by telling her that more than anything I wanted to learn from her example. From that day forward we began to spend regular time together over coffee, occasional lunches or dinners. She stood beside me as I persevered through infertility testing (her husband was my doctor, which made for awkward dinner conversations when we were all together), she encouraged me as I grappled with the challenges of full-time ministry and she comforted me as I watched my mom—who was exactly her age—pass away suddenly from cancer. Time, teaching, and tenderness are words I would definitely use to describe Marion's investment in my life. As an added bonus, six years after Bob and I moved to Austin, the Lord sent us to, what was then, the Soviet Union. At the last minute, we added Caren to our team— Marion's youngest daughter. Caren and I became fast friends, and I had a similar role in her life that her mom had in mine.

Marion is in her 70's now and suffers from Alzheimer's, and while I'm saddened by the fact that her memory is gone, I know her legacy of godliness lives on in her children's lives and my own. I'm sure countless others were touched by her teaching and example as well.

As we round the bend to the fourth chapter of II Timothy, memories of Marion have filled my mind. Her face is vivid in my memory and her voice echoes in my heart. Like Paul, she has fought the good fight of faith, she is nearing the end of the course, she has kept the faith, and in the future there is laid up for her the crown of righteousness which the Lord, the righteous Judge will award her on that day.

I want to finish well, don't you? I want to live my life in such a way that I can look forward with confidence to meeting the Lord—I hope that is true for you too. We have learned from these four chapters that in order to finish well, we must realize that following Jesus is hard, it requires suffering and sacrifice. Rather than being promised happiness, we are promised suffering. Yet, we are called to guard this treasure called the gospel, and while we protect its message we're called to entrust it to others like Marion entrusted the gospel to me, like I'm entrusting it to you.

My prayer, for me and for you, is that we will learn from Marion and Paul's example. I pray that the truth we have gleaned from this small book will inspire us to a deep-seated devotion and a lifelong pursuit of God and a willingness to follow Him wherever He leads. I also pray that you will be willing to sit across the table from that young woman who ventures to ask, "Will you disciple me?"

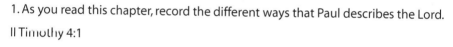

Read II Timothy

As we take a final look at this rich book of Scripture, I want you to notice that Paul, while honest and frank about his circumstances, does not despair. He is full of faith because his unwavering confidence rests in Jesus Christ. If we pause to listen, we can almost hear his voice grow louder and his fist pound harder as he exhorts Timothy, and us, to finish well.

1. As you read this chapter, record the different ways that Paul describes the Lord.

II Timothy 4:1

II Timothy 4:8

II Timothy 4:17

II Timothy 4:18

2. Paul mentions the "presence of the Lord," His "appearing" and His "kingdom" in II Timothy 4:4, 8, and18.

a. Why do you think it's significant that Paul is aware of God's presence and discusses His appearing and kingdom?

b. Describe a time when you were very aware of the Lord's presence. How did He encourage you as a result?

3. As you read these same verses, in the context of this final chapter, what does Paul say about the "future," and why do you think this gave him hope?

4. Compare these verses with the following verses and record any further insight you gain about the "future" and God's kingdom.

II Corinthians 4:16-18

Revelation 21:1-5

Revelation 22:1-5

5. As you read these three passages, what stands out to you the most and why?

Although the restored kingdom is not yet, there is something so hopeful about its reality. Tim Keller writes, "And if you know that this is not the only world, the only body, the only life you are ever going to have—that you will someday have a perfect life, a real, concrete life—who cares what people do to you? You're free from ultimate anxieties in this life, so you can be brave and take risks. You can face the worst thing...with joy, and with hope. The resurrection means we can look forward with hope to the day our suffering will be gone. But it even means that we can look forward with hope to the day our suffering will be glorious."[1]

REFLECTION

In a very real way Paul experienced the presence of God in the face of huge obstacles, great trials and significant suffering. The Lord stood with him and strengthened him as he proclaimed the gospel to the Gentiles, and at the same time, the Lord gave him hope as he looked forward to the promised kingdom. Theologians often refer to this reality as "now and not yet."

Why do you think this truth encouraged Paul and helped him to persevere?

How have you experienced God's presence in your life now?

How does the promise of His kingdom encourage you, although it is not yet?

Perhaps someone you are discipling is struggling under the weight of a heavy trial. Pray that the Lord will stand with and strengthen your friend; pray that His presence will lend comfort now; and pray that the promise of His kingdom—that place where every tear will dry and all suffering will come to an end—will give hope.

[1] Tim Keller, *King's Cross, The Story of the World in the Life of Jesus* (Dutton, New York, 2011), 224.

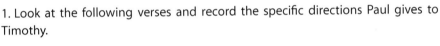

Read II Timothy

Remember that when we started our study of II Timothy we learned that this letter is Paul's "last will and testament." These are the last words he wrote to his beloved son in the faith. In fact, as we have noticed already, he refers to his exhortation as a "solemn charge." I can imagine Timothy took special note of his final words.

1. Look at the following verses and record the specific directions Paul gives to Timothy.

II Timothy 4:2

II Timothy 4:5

II Timothy 4:15

2. a. According to this next set of verses, what is Paul's motivation for these directions?

II Timothy 4:3-4

II Timothy 4:10

b. What does it mean to have our ears "tickled"? And, why do you think we are prone to bristle at the thought of "sound doctrine"?

c. Along these same lines, what are some prevalent myths among believers today that tend to ignore sound doctrine?

3. Paul exhorts Timothy to preach the word, to be ready in season and out of season (in other words, all of the time)!

a. Use **www.dictIonary.com** and look up the word "ready" and record the definition:

b. Go to the top of **www.dictionary.com** and click on "thesaurus" and write down four synonyms (different words with the same meaning) for the word *ready*.

4. Look at II Timothy 4:2 again. For what purpose are we to be ready?

REFLECTION

The past year, due to circumstances with my job, has been what I might call "off-season." I have had things to do, but in a rather unofficial capacity. I have wondered, at times, "What am I here for again? Tell me Lord, what is my purpose?" Frankly, I find it harder to "fight the fight" when things are quiet, but He has reminded me, several times, that I need to persevere just as much when I'm in the "slow lane" as I do in the middle of the fight.

We all go through seasons of life: crazy-busy, trial-filled and quiet seasons. Sometimes it is all we can do to get through the day, and other times there are not enough hours to get everything done. Paul spent a good number of years in a prison, far from "the action," and yet, we continue to learn from the Spirit-inspired words of his letters. We never know what the Lord is doing in and through our lives, but we need to be ready.

Stop and consider you current place in life. Would you describe yourself as "ready"? Why or why not?

Based upon you've learned from II Timothy, what are some practical steps you can take in order to be ready?

day three

Read II Timothy

There is fierce exhortation in this last chapter, no doubt about it. As I mentioned earlier, I can almost hear Paul's fist pounding on the table as he pens these instructions. He is dead-serious about Timothy's need to preach—in readiness. He does not mince words as he calls this young man to endure hardship, to proclaim the gospel and to fulfill his ministry. The task is clear. Yet, mingled in and through and around the edges of Paul's exhortation, we find a real person with real needs and desires, just like Timothy, you and me.

1. Read II Timothy 4:6 in the context of 4:1-8. What comes to mind when you envision a life "poured out" for others? What insight does this give you about how Paul viewed his life and ministry effort?

Over the years as I've studied the New Testament, I have been personally encouraged and strengthened by Paul's example. It is easy to think of him as nearly perfect, the apostle who endured all things, who faithfully followed Jesus through thick and thin, a man whose example is impossible to emulate. However, as I have taken the time to really read what he wrote, I see a man who needed Jesus just like I do. And, even more importantly, I see a Savior who met Paul at every turn.

2. Compare II Timothy 4:6 with the following passages and record your observations regarding Paul's humanity and his attitude toward the hardships he faced. Take note of what he says about his Savior.

Philippians 1:12-26

II Corinthians 1:3-11

II Corinthians 6:1-10

3. The following passages provide insight into Paul's understanding of the sacrifice of Jesus Christ on our behalf. To what extent did Jesus pour Himself out for us?

I Corinthians 8:1-9

Philippians 2:6-11

Hebrews 12:1-3

4. According to II Timothy 4:9, 13, 21, what are some of the things he requests of Timothy? What insight does this give you into Paul's needs?

4b. Now look at II Timothy 4:10-12, 19-21, and record the names of the men and women Paul was in touch with. What do you learn about his life and ministry?

REFLECTION

Tim Keller writes, "Why is it so hard to face suffering? Why is it so hard to face disability and disease? Why is it so hard to do the right thing if you know it's going to cost you money, reputation, maybe even your life? Why is it so hard to face your own death or the death of your loved ones? It's so hard because we think this broken world is the only world we're every going to have. It's easy to feel as if this money is the only wealth we'll ever have, as if this is the only body we'll ever have. But if Jesus is risen, then your future is so much more beautiful, and so much more certain than that."[2]

As I read these last few verses, I cannot help but think of the King and His kingdom on which Paul sets his sight, and for this reason he willingly poured out his life for the sake of the gospel. There are men and women all around us doing the work of the ministry—in their professions, neighborhoods, nursing homes, Starbucks—pouring their lives out as a drink offering, all for the sake of Jesus Christ and the hope of His kingdom. Remind a fellow believer of the beautiful future that rests on a risen Savior.

Take a few minutes to personally thank Jesus for becoming poor that you might become rich. What a gift! And, also thank Him for giving you everything you need for life and godliness (II Peter 1:2-4). At the same time, acknowledge that serving others, selflessly, is not easy nor does it come naturally. Admit your weakness and your need for Christ's love and strength. Thank Him for emptying Himself for you. Thank Him for His presence now and for the promise of His kingdom in the not yet. Ask Him for help in every area of your life—He stands by you and will strengthen you.

---

[2]Keller, 222.

day four

Read II Timothy

Whenever I watch the Olympics, I am always fascinated by the dedication displayed by the athletes. Many have practiced 14 hours a day, for several years, in order to compete in the games. Only a select few return home with a medal; most will never receive a reward for their hard work. When I watch runners compete for the prize, I always notice that they do not slow down until after they cross the finish line. As believers we need to exercise a similar kind of discipline and hard work, not to earn God's love, but to bring glory to His name. It really matters how we live and also how we finish. What matters most is that Jesus finished well. He fought the battle over sin and death and won! He sits at the right hand of the Father. His Spirit lives in you and me, giving us everything we need to run the race, fight the good fight of faith and to finish well.

Today, as we wrap up our study of II Timothy, we are going to focus on finishing well. I encourage you to pray as you begin your time with the Lord, asking Him to give you a heart to listen and respond.

Look at I Corinthians 9:19-27 to answer the following questions.

1. First, record what you notice about Paul's attitude toward the gospel and those to whom he preaches in 9:19-23.

2. His commitment to making the gospel relevant and accessible is challenging, don't you agree? In order to proclaim the gospel, these kinds of sacrifice are often necessary. Describe how you choose to "become all things to all men" for the sake of the gospel.

3. I feel really uncomfortable just writing these questions! I hate to admit it, but I squirm at the thought of being inconvenienced for the sake of Christ. I often pray for my neighbors, but I have to think twice about inviting them over for dinner. I have too many important things to do. I am challenged by Paul's example and I'm asking myself with every letter typed, "Do I fully grasp the importance of the gospel message? Am I willing to sacrifice my schedule, my to-do list for the sake of His name?" I want to be. I am well aware that sometimes discipleship begins with sharing the gospel, seeing someone come to Christ and taking him/her to the next step. Today I realize that the first step starts with my willingness to be used. What about you?

4. Read I Corinthians 9:24-27. Paul uses the metaphor of a runner and a boxer to explain the believer's attitude toward the gospel and the Christian life. How does he describe:

Those who run to win:

The difference between the spiritual and physical prize awarded:

A winning boxer:

5. How would you describe your current position in the race? Are you disciplined, motivated, and focused, or distracted, uncertain, lethargic? What steps might you take to run in such a way that you may win? Talk to the Lord about how you are feeling.

My purpose in looking at this passage is not to put you under another pile. It is not to beat you into spiritual shape. My purpose is to remind you that it takes discipline and effort to run with endurance. Life, for most of us, is not a sprint but a long-distance race. The older I get, the more often I hear stories about men and women of the faith who, for a variety of reasons, have been disqualified. Sometimes it is moral failure, other times it is financial impropriety, and/or some have simply walked away from the faith. As I have moved into my 50's, I am much more aware of the fact that the finish line is getting closer. I have realized that if I want to finish well, which I do, it will take an equal amount of perseverance and discipline. I cannot coast. Neither can you.

REFLECTION

As you finish this study, pull out your Personal Development Plan. Reexamine the areas that you plan to focus on during this season in your life. Are there any adjustments you would like to make as you finish your study of II Timothy? Let me encourage you to begin laying a foundation for your future walk with the Lord today. If you are discipling someone, share your plan and ask for prayer. If someone is mentoring you, share your plan and ask for prayer.

Read II Timothy...one last time.

The following questions are taken from the first four days and will be used for discussion in your group.

1. Stop and consider you current place in life. Would you describe yourself as "ready"? Why or why not?

2. Based upon you've learned from II Timothy, what are some practical steps you can take in order to be ready?

3. What does it mean to have our ears "tickled" And, why do you think we are prone to bristle at the thought of "sound doctrine"?

4. Along these same lines, what are some prevalent myths among believers today that tend to ignore sound doctrine?

5. How would you describe your current position in the race? Are you disciplined, motivated, and focused, or distracted, uncertain, lethargic? What steps might you take to run in such a way that you may win? Talk to the Lord about how you are feeling.

6. As you finish, pull out your Personal Development Plan. Re-examine the areas that you plan to focus on during this season in your life. Are there any adjustments you would like to make as a result of finishing your study of II Timothy? Let me encourage you to include spiritual disciplines on the list. Begin laying a foundation for your future walk with the Lord today. If you are discipling someone, share your plan and ask for prayer. If someone is mentoring you, share your plan and ask for prayer. Remember discipleship takes place both ways! You can learn as much from those you are discipling as they learn from you.

You have now completed six weeks of an intense look at II Timothy and the subject of discipleship. In addition to reflecting on your PDP, take some time to reflect on what you have learned and how the Lord has challenged you to follow Him in a deeper and fuller way. Now, take what you have learned and heard, in the presence of many witnesses, and entrust it to faithful followers of Jesus that they may teach others also. Make discipleship - discipling others and being discipled a way of life!

Bibliography

Bartholomew, Craig, Michael Goheen. *The True Story of the Whole World: Finding Your Place in the Biblical Drama.* Grand Rapids, MI, 2004.

Beale, G.K., Carson, D.A. *Commentary on the New Testament Use of the Old Testament.* Grand Rapids, MI: Baker Academic, 2007.

Bonhoeffer, Dietrich. *Dietrich Bonheoffer—Discipleship Vol. IV.* Augsburg Fortress, 2005.

Bonhoeffer, Dietrich. *Life Together.* New York, NY: Harper Collins Publishing, 1954.

Carson, D.A. *New Bible Commentary, 21st Century Edition, 4th Ed. (II Timothy 2:1-7).* Downers Grove, IL, 1994.

Draper, James T., Keathley, Kenneth. *Biblical Authority: The Critical Issue for the Body of Christ.* Nashville, TN: Broadman & Holleman, 2001.

Erickson, Millard J. *Postmodernizing the Faith.* Grand Rapids, MI: Baker Books, 1998.

Greear, J.D. *Gospel, Recovering the Power that Made Christianity Revolutionary.* Nashville, TN: B&H Publishing, 2011.

Keller, Timothy *The King's Cross: The Story of the World in the Life of Jesus.* New York, NY, 2011.

Lyons, Gabe. *The Next Christians: How A Generation is Restoring the Faith.* New York.NY: Doubleday, 2010.

Peterson, Eugene. *Eat This Book.* Grand Rapids: MI, 2006.

Stott, John *II Timothy: Stand in Truth.* Downers Grove, IL: InterVarsity Press, 1998.

Made in the USA
San Bernardino, CA
03 July 2017